BOMB

poems

Ashley Inguanta

"To open this book is to enter the yearning of an uncommon angel, one who envisions the extraordinary in the ordinary, who sees how loss opens to love, how the natural world infuses cities with magic. Geese, coyotes, and roses share the space with glittering human-made lights. At once, though you may see the "Shutter, pressed" and "Life, suspended," there is the movement of scattering seeds, the earth turning beneath those stars. When the world drops us, it catches us again. This poet navigates a landscape of tangible mirage and dreams in which letting go and merging become one and the same. There is so much light here, in everything, mapping a way for us through ache." —DARLIN' NEAL, *Elegant Punk*

"You will feel chills throughout your entire body. Read this book." —FRANCESCA LIA BLOCK

"Ashley Inguanta's *Bomb* explodes across the page, rendering to rubble what we think we understand about love, loss, and the self. Calling out to the ghost of Amelia Earhart and other "unbearable angels" of the American West, Inguanta guides us through the devastation with a voice that is both deeply vulnerable and wildly free. What else is there to say? I loved this book." —MONICA WENDEL

"Ashley Inguanta's new collection of poems Bomb is an evocative meditation on the force of love's explosive nature. Inguanta uses precise line and form to reveal a reverent, embodied experience with gorgeously layered images and metaphors to remind the reader of love's familiar tendency to immolate. She maps the terrain of her poetry with cities, buildings, roads, and regions. Love is cartography as well as prayer and a lament. It is destructive, transformative, creative, anguished, passionate, quiet, and still. The lover and the beloved are often voiced as women, but not always. This collection is Inguanta's heart. *Bomb* is so beautiful."

—APRIL BRADLEY, Associate Editor of *Bartleby Snopes Literary Magazine* and Founding Editor of *Women Who Flash Their Lit*

BOMB

poems

AMPERSAND BOOKS
www.ampersand-books.com

ISBN: 978-0-9861370-5-1

Cover design by: Matthew Revert
Typesetting by: Jeremy John Parker
Photograhy by: Ashley Inguanta
Modeling by: Tara Michelle Young

The publisher would like to thank: The usual suspects and unusual culprits, WOW Airlines, Delta Airlines, RyanAir, Google, CapitalOne, Gutenburg, Bernie Sanders, bloody wolves, our own infinite patience, red pandas, giant pandas, any and all other pandas, Radiohead, Montreal, miles of highways, miles of skies, Amsterdam, orchids, blue hydrangeas, bullet trains to anywhere, coffee, Facebook, Lana del Rey (again), and Wild Scandinavian Silkyfoxes.

TABLE OF CONTENTS

For anyone who has ever been left behind,
who understands miraculous rhythm, the tick-tick,

the way love brings its hands to you, attaches
the wires, sets the timer

and then—when the clock hits zero, vanishes,
just in time

for you to lose access to something great
inside of you.

I am here to tell you that you will find it again.

PLACE YOUR HAND ON HER THIGH

CONNECT THE WIRES

MOVE YOUR PALM UP, OVER HER BELLY
UNDERNEATH HER LEFT BREAST

LISTEN TO THE TICK

TICK

TICK

NOW
MAKE YOUR WAY
TO THE HEART

AND LOVE HER

AND LISTEN

YOU MUST LISTEN

AND YOU MUST LOVE HER

AND YOU DO

YOU DO

DEDICATION: TO THE ONE I WILL MARRY

Not long after a friend tells me about her mother—how she, at 7, lost her father in World War II, how she learned to live with his ghost, the love he could not give—I see a coyote in the night, running below a billboard for $12 roses. I wonder, if all this world's lonely people could fit roses into the stories of our bodies, tell me: Will the woman I marry come down from a future's heaven and place each petal in my mouth, a kiss?

Will we all heal when heaven meets flower?
Will I find miracle when her finger presses my tongue?
Will she make her way here—worn from her travel
through time—
hungry and tired, wanting my love
the way I have always wanted to find something wild
and rare and lone, traveling
like a warrior through the night?

I found a warrior once.
Gun in hand, she ran towards me
like a soldier searching for peace.
She said, "We've been through battle."

She said, "I love you."
And then she was gone.

And let me tell you, I've wandered through America
holding the hand of such an unbearable angel.

Maybe one day she will shoot for the Earth, and I'll
catch her golden bullet between my teeth, finding its
place as an egg in a nest of roses.

Then, a woman from the future will wear a ring that
matches mine.
And maybe, just maybe, in this version I will not
catch the bullet after all.

Maybe this woman, this new woman, she will open
me like an oyster, holding
the cluster of roses—bullet dead center—in her hands.

Maybe she will place this gift deep between my
lungs, pound my heart into place again.

Maybe she will follow right after, bare and open—a
miracle.

Maybe she will become a coyote in the night.

Maybe she will become the thing that shapes each
bomb inside of me.

BEFORE IT BREAKS

I wanted to draw you in charcoal. Instead, you became a subway train, its smoke and noise. You fed me honey in a poem once, and I ate from the spoon you held as carefully as a flower. You are dusk. You are the grey heat that rises from underground. You are the curve of metal on track. And as I sit, wishing I could see more than the underground, you step like an angel. I imagine you running, wet concrete from rain. The smell of your hair. The way you may or may not look up. The way you may or may not order coffee, the way you may or may not sit by your favorite window, watching the city become glitter golden light. The way you may or may not start a fire, yearning to become something else. I want to find you in the map this city has dug itself. I wonder, if I could find you, if you would open your eyes, if you would become a miracle. Sometimes I imagine us in an apartment we never had—empty, except for one bed, and there is a camera in the corner. You stand, I sit. You hold berries, I eat. You see the window and see yourself as glass. I empty like a spider egg, hatched. You close the shutter with the machine in the palm of your hand. And then, more quickly than you can imagine, all will burn to white.

I

EACH BOMB INSIDE OF ME

WHEN ALL THE WARS IN THIS WORLD

The night after they found two white flags
on the Brooklyn Bridge,

I sit at home alone. When I place
my hand between my legs, I see

the flags, your face. I love you, still.
I love you still, and I want you

to know when all the wars
in this world
peak in their emptiness

and light, I will be there
to make sure you are safe,

to make sure you can see it all,
all sprawled out like a map.

A star here, Earth there,
your hands on my belly, your mouth
on my neck.

And then explosion.

And then nothing.

THE DAY THEY FOUND

a piece of Amelia Earhart's plane,
you dream of your mother—
she is dying, and you are holding
her in your arms.

The women you've loved, the one you almost married,
they are there, too—in the lines on your hands, heart
etched deeply into a body you did not create, but
were given.

I do not know why flowers need scientific names,
or why airplanes fall apart, or why we must wait
among the ocean waves for a lifeboat, or why
she had to leave, or why people die in dreams.

I only know this: We all have been
interrupted in some way.

The metal wing, the angel
falling down, through windows,
ready to hold your hand, the rescue
you hoped would never have to come.

FLOWER GIRL

Last year, I delivered flowers
in Brooklyn,

and the woman I once loved, she never cried
in front of me. I would realize this months later

in Florida, when I finally came home.

There, I would see a white horse in the St. John's
and whisper a prayer to the sky.

In Brooklyn, I stepped toe-first into puddles of rain
with roses in my hands.

A woman answered the door
looking worn, simple—
like a paper bag.

These are for you, I said.
How kind, she said.

And the night glittered, a starry hymnal,
a cluster of space, holding
all I could not.

DON'T ASK QUESTIONS

I'm talking to you: The woman
who makes origami cities,
sells them in subway tunnels.

After months of winter, Spring seemed
impossible, like wishing for a bird to return
after letting it loose. But today,
as I guided the wings of your paper crane
over the Empire State, something changed—
a slice of heat against my palm, a sliver
of golden light curving underground.

You have made paper cities without paper people,
and I have written one million poems about
loneliness,
about birds fluttering like comets into thin air.

Instead of asking the price of a skyscraper,
I wish for you to be kind,

and you are, and the flowers have never
opened so fast after winter,

blooming above us—
a breaking heart,
a lover waiting.

THE FIRST WORD

of suicide came that morning, on our way
to homeroom. We did not know her,
but we saw her, nearly every day,
beautiful in what was, to us, mystery,
and in that moment when you said, "She hung
herself,"
my body opened like a cavern—an echo
grew and tumbled, a voice.

I spent the rest of the day in the library, occasionally
going to class. I may have been reading Shakespeare,
hiding in my secret spot, writing poems about a
woman far,
always a woman far,

and I was in love but could not admit it,
with a girl who was becoming, we were all girls
becoming—
and on that day, gone was gone was gone.

I returned home and my mother asked me what
happened.
I told her.

I went to my room and my body opened—not
blossom, but root.

DEDICATION: TO THE REGISTRAR

Years ago, I wrote a poem before boarding an airplane.

A dream of mine: When I was a young girl, I held my grandfather's hand, and we ran. I was a monster, growing. He had the greenest eyes. I remember ghosts. I remember how—after the poem, after the dream—I turned to gold when I kissed the woman I loved, when I kissed her hair. I remember when I thought all of this made sense once, when I drove past palm trees and all things wild. It is in my DNA to love hard.

I am telling this to you because you have seen the way my DNA can spiral, and I want you to take me home.

So listen: The dream of my grandfather. There is another man who has never showed up in any of my dreams, but he is also my blood. He had a scar between his eyes. Tell me—when you saw him, when you marked down his features, when you scanned his face—did you see a young girl forming from his

DNA, from those lines, from his dark complexion, from the scar between his eyes? I want to know, how did he speak to you? He filled out his draft card, World War II. His body belonged to America. Did he know of this belonging, how this new country would now hold his body in its arms? Tell me.

Tell me this, and I will tell you that in my dream, my body belonged to the place all good dreamers go: Into the sky, looking down from an airplane window, maybe at clouds or maybe at matchbox homes. I held the hand of someone safe. I was made from this safety, but I am also made from something hard. Muscle, tan. A scar that belongs to body, a body that belongs to a country that has just been born.

1942, April. That's when you saw my great grandfather, when he spoke to you, when he told you his birthday, when you noticed what he was made of.

Tell me: Did you feel it? The seed of yourself? Were these roots spreading like a river? Did he speak like someone who has traveled far, like someone who knew what was coming?

And was I there, too? Tell me. Was I there?

I SEE YOU THERE IN BLACK AND WHITE,

mushroom cloud blooming. We are on set, are nothing but a dream—you and your friends in slow motion. And I—maybe I was the photographer, a ghost in the wall, a beam of color that just couldn't get out, or maybe that was you—all hidden-bright, like secret lovers or a woman who has been told to stop mourning, enough is enough.

That evening, before the bomb, I went to an all-night bodega on my walk home. I felt cold, like a metal rod, or like a snowflake, or like the ocean. I hummed a song my grandmother used to sing. A butterfly, a cigarette. A big white puff of smoke coming down the road. Magic, my hands. And you—maybe you are the rabbit. Maybe you are the feathered trick up my sleeve. Maybe you are the heart that beats deep inside of me. Maybe you are map, unfolding, dream-state electric.

II

IF I BECOME A GHOST

IN A SIMPLER TIME

we gave glass bottles to the sea, hoping
that one day our stories would be found, heard.

Alone now, I listen to the radio: Pigeons have been
delivering messages in India. Our phone conversations
are discussed as sacred. I drink coffee, headed
to the airport. I will be flying to the Deep South to read
stories of two women who once loved each other, who
could not make it across the sea, who could not find
a bird who would listen. No matter how many times
these women said, "Please, someone must remember
us," the world turned on. Neither wave nor wing
could save them. And the telephone—it became
a bright invention, but it could not save them.

And maybe that is the point.
Maybe their story does not belong to the world.

The world, spinning like a ballerina, or like a tornado,
would not know what to do with such silence.

IF I BECOME A GHOST

I will wrap you. I will sing to you
a lullaby, in tune, and repeat to you
stories you've told me
over and over
about your childhood,
how you grew up strong,
and finally, finally landed
into the place I would find you.

I will tell you this story of finding,
and you will tell me new stories
of roses, of the way the Earth turns,
of the way you continue to make
your coffee and talk to me
through the thick Florida air.

I will be there
reminding you that something beautiful has come,
that something beautiful
is on its way.

TO BE THE HOUSES

I remember buildings—homes, a parking lot. My
car. The heat. Myself alone or not alone—it doesn't
matter—and darkness, so much of it, that when
I'd pull onto the main road it looked like a storm
of stars. This town is the Last of the South and
sometimes, when I want to remember, I will drive
into the light, past the gas station and the sandwich
shop and the place where I wanted to kiss you, and
God, someone has to listen to this story, someone
must know that last night, when I pulled onto this
town's main road everything sparkled bigger than
ever, like New York City, or like the way your bare
body folds and opens underneath golden light. I
took a turn, tunneled into shadow.

What if I told you that I am the shadow?
What if I told you that the tunnel isn't fast enough?
What if I told you that I am the storm?

And what if I told you I long to be the houses?

I am not the houses but

What if

What if I long to be?

SOUTH

When life is nothing but a dream
of the cool Carolina night, you write me a letter
from your place in the city. I sit on a dock
far away, underneath a bowl of starlight.
The water below moves like an oily, black wing
just before takeoff. The neighbors shout 'Merica
and dive in. I roll a cigarette, look up. I want to tell you
something beautiful, like there is a miracle coming.

But instead the moon fades, and in the morning,
when I make my way through the streets of
Charleston,
I grow to understand that I am without you
in this world,
that I am simply a woman walking on cobblestones
with a basket of greens, Chanel on my
wrists, cigarette
between my fingers, dirt on my feet.

Here, a bird takes off.

I feel my body flatten into horizon.

IN ONE OF MY MANY DREAMS OF LOVE

I felt my ovaries empty, and I became hungry.

In this dream I was hungry, and it was storming, so I
caught a fish: Small, modest, silver,
like the earrings of a woman who is ready to loosely
tie up her hair, show herself.

In this dream of love, I could not remember a time
storm had yielded to such necessity:

The smooth sky of night,
the way we gasp as steam rises,
thin over water. The way I say
Here is my neck, here is my breast
here is my heart. The way that,
when it's my time to move on, I step
into a cool lagoon, my body eggless and hollow,
the sky drumming down—one beat, two—
and I cannot see anything but

one thousand fish weaving through sheets of rain.

All of this heartbreaking beauty—where does it go
when we wake? What did we have to give up
in order to get here? A room full of lifelong friends?
Tomatoes, growing on the vine? A belly full
of minnows? A kiss warm and soft?

Go on, I say, *Close your eyes*
and imagine this: Two gentle hands
on your abdomen. Breathe.

COUNTY LINE POEM

I love too many people, but I do not know how
to love too many people. That will be my downfall,
and let me tell you, as I walk down to the street
from my new country home, I understand
that we are all flawed, that the sunset cannot
save us from ourselves, from the way we love
and love and love and love.

Next door, an old man keeps his dog out.
The dog guards the driveway, the grass.

One street over, and the county line is drawn.

I wonder who in this holy world would dare
cross such a divide: Man and dog, woman
and road. The country is a new stretch
of peace and of open shortcomings. Here,

in this landscape, nothing can hide. Your life,
there, in front of you, saying "please," saying

"See me, I am here. I am the grass,
I am the hill," and I want to know

what happens when Earth closes its eyes
it can no longer see the moon, but feel it

like a loved one twirling, moving away,
moving towards,
a reckless but steady orbit, a glow, a tug of wind.

AT MY GRANDMOTHER'S FUNERAL, I IMAGINED HOLDING HANDS WITH THE WOMAN I ONCE LOVED

What do you do
when your lover leaves you for the wolves?

Do you listen to the way
seasons change? The way patterns form,
the way your grandmother, her mother, become
one voice, deepened, when the root passes? What do
you do
when your lover leaves you for the wolves
as root passes?

Do you listen, do you gather?
Do you sing?
Do you hold heaven in your hands
and beg your palms to bring something kind
into your fortune?

Do you place your hands to the Earth and say,
"become, become"?

I listened to one sister say goodbye to the other.
I was alone here.
The sister leaned over the other's coffin, whispered
something sweet into her ear.

When there was nothing more to say,
the floor dropped. I fell into a place
where I would ask no more questions.

I would not care to know what to do.
There would be no way out.

IN ANOTHER TIME, I WOULD HAVE TAKEN THE WOMAN I LOVED TO SICILY

We are in the sky together, and when I tell her stories
of my great-grandfather, my family, she looks out

the airplane window, golden light on her face,
her silk blouse shining like a mirage.

She says, "I see them out there
in the clouds," and in this innocent

view of heaven, I understand
her beauty, her grace

the way her palms open, as vulnerable
as a new country. In this innocence,
she is ready to hold both my hands.

This may have happened in another time,
but who am I to say what we would have done?

Did my great grandfather know
that he would become a mystery?

In the story of another time, our plane lands.
She lifts her suitcase, and the moon teaches us to craft
lace. In the story of myself alone, I have a passport
and it is empty. It is beautiful, glistening
as I carry it in my purse. I carry it everywhere,

and I use it to hold marigolds, sunflower seeds.
On the day flowers grow from my spine, they will
turn to ink.

YOU LOVE HER

AND YOU BOTH KNOW

THAT BLESSINGS MAKE THE BOMB

THE TICK

TICK

TICK

CLIMAXES

MAKE THE BOMB

ORCHIDS

NESTS

MAKE THE BOMB

THE MOVEMENT OF SUBWAY CARS,
THE WAY

THEY CURVE AND SPARK

THE NOURISHMENT OF
BERRIES, WHEAT

MAKES THE BOMB

THE WAY YOU MOVE
INSIDE OF EACH OTHER

WITH GRACE
AND ADMIRATION

MAKES THE BOMB

YOU LOVE HER

SHE SAYS SHE IS IN PAIN

THAT HER HEART IS SO LOUD
SHE CANNOT STAND IT

AND YOU LISTEN

AND YOU SAY, I AM IN PAIN TOO

BUT I LOVE YOU

AND I AM SORRY

DEDICATION:
TO THOSE WHO WANT
IT ALL TO END

When you wake, tell me, does each bird still sing?

When you wake, tell me, how do you move on?

Tell me this, and I will tell you the only reason
I want to believe in something greater is because
when I walk to the river I still hear nothing,
and when I call, no cardinals come, no sparrows,
no jays. But if you hear the birds, if you can step
into the music, then maybe, just maybe

there is warmth there for all of us, celestial, and oh
how the sun will shine on our feet
brushing each leaf, on our knees
meeting earth, on our palms
following, hallelujah, onto winter's ground.

THE WOMAN WHO MADE THE EARTH ERUPT

It is her first night in this Texas town, and the lightning bugs are dancing over flooded streets. Something deep has exploded within the earth. She wonders if she will ever be kissed again, truly lovingly.

When she walks through the water on the street, it moves like a river—a sweet, unbearable breaking of the road. She waits for answers. She steps through the flood, towards the fire trucks, into the light—deep and red and flickering like an angel.

The neighbors come out of their homes, holding buckets. One by one, they gather water, walk back inside. The woman, she sees something small, something bright—an opening, right there, right there. She brings her body to it. She almost touches it, almost.

There is a freedom that comes when someone kind lets go of your hand.

III

TO WAKE NEAR AN UNBEARABLE ANGEL

ATLANTIC

Her belief in God astounded me
in the same way a river would press to a woman
who has spent her whole life wading
in one pond, kissing the surface.

Everything made sense to me then, in that room,
in the boathouse, waiting for kingdom come,
waiting for her to touch me, all rugged
elegance, a cowgirl with scars.

When she unbuttoned my shirt, unclasped
my bra, she cupped my breasts, wrapped my wrists
with her hands. She butterflied into a whisper,
fit her body into mine.

She smelled like spices, honey.
Her skin was the warmth of God's home.
She moved like a lion.

I brought her into bloom,
and then rest,

the lightening of body,
no longer stone.

ROADMAP

I.
I begin in New York. Tropical
Florida opens next, where I become
a wild horse in the St. John's.

Both wish and my love for you
bring me to Carolina, and soon
a flock of birds will move me West,
where I cross a bridge
over the Rio Grande Gorge
and turn to prairie, restoring
in wide open space.

I move this way
for quite some time:
East, North, South, West.

I don't know about all hearts,
but I can speak for my own:

If I were to be held again,
I may break.

Please be careful.
Please.

I say this to you and I say this to myself.

II.
At the end of things, as we are now, tell me:
Are you as sad and angry as you were in that dream?

I said goodbye,
and you said goodbye.

And we cycled.

If the cluster of birdsong
is the echo of a woman gone,
then I can assure you, all parting
will be done with such purpose,
such love.

III.
A long time ago, I read a story
of our becoming:

The world began at one point—a place
where all was pressed flat. Endings
and beginnings were nothing but myths,

and bodies thinly connected to voices,
discovering how express love.

When Mrs. Ph(i)Nk_0 longed for room
to cook noodles for the boys, when
she said, "... ah, what noodles, boys!"[1]
the world expanded, planets formed.

Tonight, I left the grocery with fresh greens
and spaghetti, and in a thick pocket of silence,
the clerk almost touched my hand.

I wanted to cook for her.
I wanted to kiss her.

I wanted to ask,
Do you like working here?

But instead, I went home
and tucked myself into clean sheets.

I imagined leaving, moving
to a remote town: Coyotes in the dusk,
flower blooming from cow skull,
tubs of bath water cooling in the twilight,
roads long and dry—one thick stack

1. From Italo Calvino's "All At One Point"

of cash in my hand, renting yet another room,
checking out groceries,
working the night shift,
asking everybody

How are you?

over and over, riding home
underneath crisp starlight.

Here, no one would know me.
I could become a stone in skin.
I could become everything I never was:
a bird in flight, everybody's angel,
until the truth comes out,
— my heart, a diamond —
sharp and clear, cut
by my own reckless hand.

But you once told me that forgiveness
is a kiss, on forehead, and when I read
my nightly poem, I hear your voice,

and it's not for describing on paper.

The whole block falls quiet, dark.

I WANDERED THROUGHOUT AMERICA WITH AN UNBEARABLE ANGEL

And she held my hand. When I cupped
her breast in my palm, she read me
a new story of creation:

There is a woman, and she's
walking into something
greater, a pocket of air,
eye of the storm, the hollow
twang of southern night.

She stops at the gas station
and stand in line. The clerk
says, "How are you?"

She speaks to him like a church bell,
or like a snake, or like a heroine
in a movie. And in the story, when it is my turn
to buy cigarettes, I fish for a dime
underneath bright lights.

I say, to the angel: I long to be alone in dust.
I long for light and space, the heart
that pieces together storm—

three parts thunder
and one part stone.

BURIAL

At a baseball game in Santa Fe, the prairie told me a secret. It was full, like lungs swelling with dirt, roots. I grabbed at it and ran into a vision of my father, the moon, uncurling a rope for me; I run up into his light, and he's telling me *All girls grow, all girls grow*, and the air is soft—like Prairie's hands, like my breathing—and it is then I understand why dogs walk on all fours, why our legs are important, why I said yes when she crawled inside of my mouth, scared and hiding like a sheep, wanting me to rescue her, lovingly, like Mary did; *but I am not Mary* I say, and my father, he is still there, large and glowing moon, and my body—my body is heavy stone sinking water, food for sheep, clay apple, and I believe Prairie when she touches me, her fingers sliding deep into my body, a wish for me to become, become. I believe Prairie when she says, *Shhh, girl*, and when she says, *No one knows how beautiful the sky is here. No one.* But we know. I touch Prairie's cheek, she hums, her throat as worn as a dog's. My legs are sore. I look up and see purple, red—falling onto the moon, falling onto her hands—and the rope my father uncurled, it's loose now, swinging;

and my body, it's growing, and I don't stop it. I run far, far away from this sky no one but we three have seen. I am heavy with water, with roots. My feet are big as satellites. I will not tell a thing. Not a thing.

DEDICATION: TO ALL THAT STEPS UNDERGROUND

You run, wet concrete from rain.
And when the poem gains its footing, you look up.

When you open your eyes, when you become a miracle,
and you bring a match to its place in the book.

You strike it.

The world lights up.

You become something else.

WE ARE ONLY GIVEN SO MUCH TIME

I am reminded of this as the airplane
takes off, the way wing and air
press to fly. I will be going to your city,
but you will have moved on.

In the morning, when I wake
in my friend's apartment, I will be
alone. I will roam from living room
to bedroom in search of light,

and when I finally make it,
when I finally press fingertip
to window glass, I will be reminded
of how delicate Brooklyn is
underneath it all: The graffiti
and ice and steel. One slip
of the tongue can lead
to kiss. One drop
of a hand can lead
to the joining
of body and body

soul and soul
until you
say

Our time is out.
I no longer know what love is.

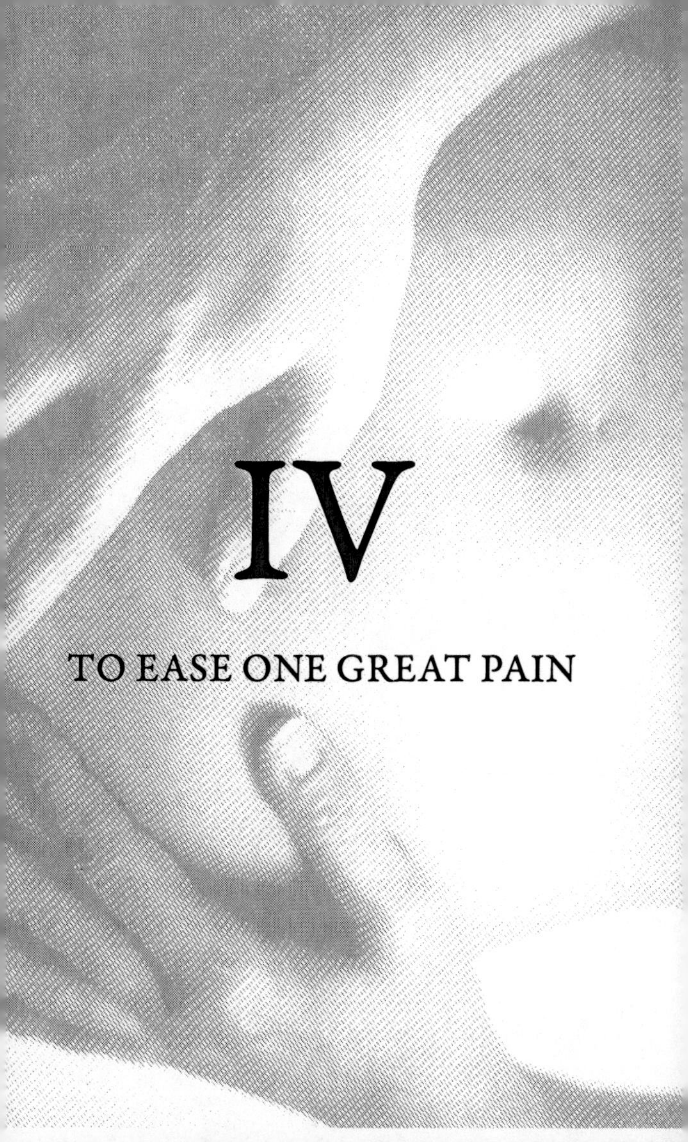

IV

TO EASE ONE GREAT PAIN

LAST NIGHT IN A DREAM

Last night in a dream, I was healthy. You were a rose.
You got into my car and I took you home, and when
you saw the white flags at the Brooklyn bridge's
arc, you told me the story of a conflicted hero, all
shadow and moon, and I told you a story about
resurrecting the dead. In your story, the hero did not
want to die, so she did not leap. Instead, she turned
into a seed. In my story, I kneeled by your grave.
When I heard gunfire, I dodged each bullet—and
then, finally, I woke up next to you, all new, stripes
of sunlight over your hair like a crisp photograph.

Sometimes I wonder: If God could really hear me,
what would the moon do? Any good moon would
reach over both white flags, carry them to you as you
fall asleep. Any good moon would hold me here, in
this dream, where I can run to you without losing
my breath, where you are a rose and my heart is
good as new.

FAITH STORY

I.

I don't want to erase anything: The way we caught a cab, mid-snowfall, the way you folded into the city as the sun set. If I had a choice, I would not forget the way that—before I pressed my fingers along your spine—I traveled West, into the desert, like a pilgrim, and shared noodles with a homeless man before I finally found a place to rest. I would not erase the way I shared this moment with you, in a letter, my words prayers. When I lost you, the Earth leveled and split. I didn't know what to do, so I made a wish. The tides rushed in.

They say bodies change when a lover leaves. I am now an earthquake, a thunderstorm. I imagine you at your window, a tornado spinning golden light.

In the distance, a wild horse bolts.

II.

Even further now, different versions of us: You sit up straight, ready. I hold your hand. A dove appears inside your palm, and you arc your body like a bridge splitting over water. I place my hand on your thigh. Hundreds of years ago, you once told me, we fought in battle. And then we became seeds. You, a cherry blossom and I, a willow.

And now, with your body curved and stretched, I release first. The dove becomes a hurricane. You say, *shh*, place your palm over its eye. I rest my head on your heart, a totem. You hold the small of my back.

A stampede builds from dust.
The one who created us lights a candle.

The dread of each animal becomes flower.

III. THROUGH YET ANOTHER WAR

I say *hold on*, softly, as to ease one great pain before we must go.

When I open my eyes again, I am a newborn crying on wet terrain, and you are the light coming through each leaf, each window. As I grow older, you reveal your shape. I remember now: How my body opened like a rose, how your hand held me, from the inside, how you felt soft and pink as a seashell, how—when I pressed my ear to your belly—I heard the ocean through your body.

And when I understand I am becoming a new woman in a new time, I long to tell you of a dream I had: We are in a house, and a big city holds us. Someone new meets me by the staircase; she wants to cook for me. You warm the room and she says *The sun is so beautiful today*. When she kisses me, you stay.

You hold the root of each tree and provide food. You visit us when we become tired, weary, worn. You bring your new body—this light—to the lip of land that breaks Earth apart.

And when my lover and I are old, you will be there,
bringing us through yet another war.

We will remember every softness
as the one missile, built to destroy everything,
takes us into the next life.

YOU REMEMBER A TIME

YOU FED HER HONEY ON A SPOON

AND BY UNDERSTANDING
THE CURVATURE OF HER MOUTH

YOU CREATE A WAVE
TO HOLD HER

THE WIRES THAT RUN
FROM THIGH TO HEART

ARE IN PLACE

AND YOU UNDERSTAND

THE WAY HER HEART BEATS

IT SOUNDS JUST AS BEAUTIFUL

AS YOUR OWN

WHEN IT BREAKS

DEDICATION: FOR THOSE WHO COULD NOT LET GO

You don't have to understand,
but look anyway. There, in the ocean.
The back of something great peeking
from the surface. It's not a shark,
so don't worry. It's not a dolphin
either, so don't expect it to leap
from the ocean like a miracle.

You understand others notice too,
and they point, speak to each other.

You are alone. You wonder if this
Great Something is hurt, unable
to swim. Maybe you are seeing
a whale, something colossal
roaming under the surface.

A manatee, you think.

"It's a sea turtle!" Someone shouts.

And, like that, an answer.

You don't know if it's the truth.
It doesn't matter.

You walk into the water, clear
and tropical, and know
that you are home,
that it's okay.

Go ahead, swim out.
When a wave comes, dive under.

FOR CONSIDERATION

They say to be kind, patient —
but if you wait too long
with open palms, the arrival
might slip from your hands.

And if you meet a person
with a cold heart, what appears
as stone may actually be
a shell
with something precious
underneath.

Be weary of those who say, "push."
Sometimes the best you can do
is leave it alone.

Be careful not to mistake self-hatred
for humbleness — you do not know
whose life you can save.

And when the day breaks
remember
not to miss any of it.

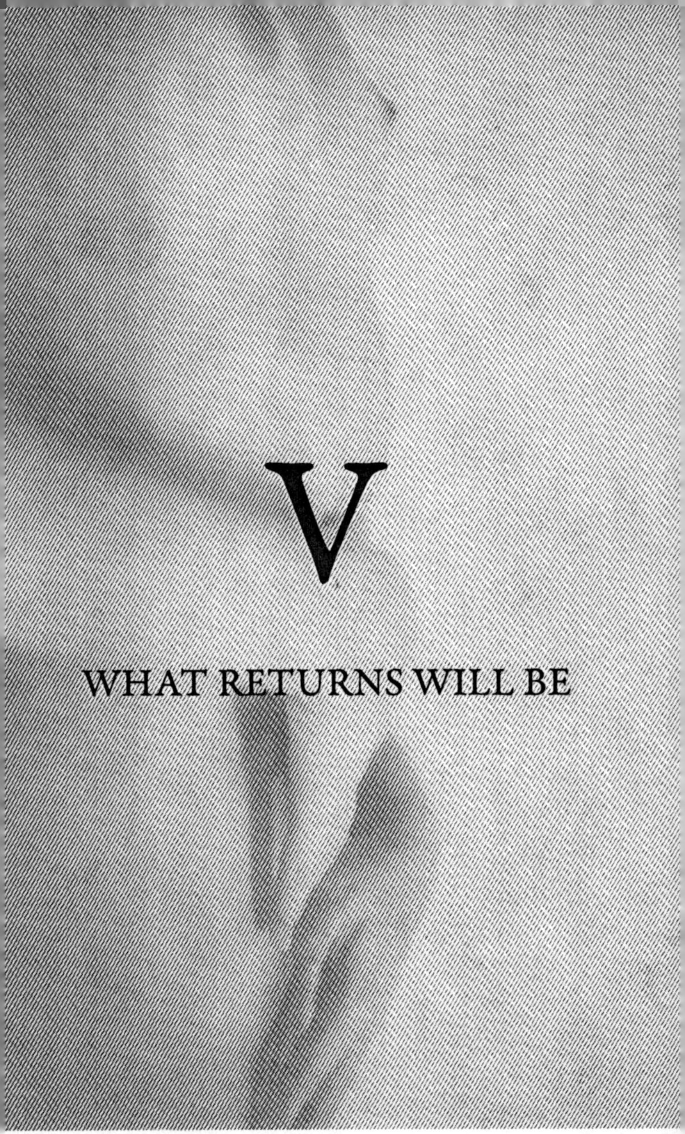

V

WHAT RETURNS WILL BE

I WAS NEVER AFRAID TO DREAM

just like my fire-lieutenant father
as he captured an image
iconic to his time: Cat on a hot tin roof,
New York City, 1972.

He tells the story with assurance.
He says, I was off duty.
He says, the building was all holy hell,
all fire and smoke.
The cat just leapt, he says.
I had my camera on me, he says.

Almost every paper wanted this photograph.
It was that simple. That clear.

Sometimes, I wonder
if the timing of love
walks the same precise
line as shutter, pressed
and life, suspended.

And if it does, tell me, where are you?
Are you the tight-rope queen?

Are you the star of Cony Island?
And when you go to bed, do you feel
a missing space? Do you understand

that I have been waiting my whole life
to fall beside you? To become
a better version of me?

IF I WERE AMELIA EARHART

Because I've thought about it,
because I went way down,
I cannot be a pilot.
It's in the books—
an automatic disqualification.

A friend tells me this
as we walk on the Lower East Side in the rain.
The brick buildings remind me of California,
the redwoods on our hike together
years ago. I remember their deep color,
blankets of clover growing, how hope
filled each space with root, with leaf.

Then I knew of a brilliant love,
but could not touch it. And now that I have,
and now that it has slipped, now that I can't find
you,
I wonder what it would be like
to go up, up up—by my own hand—
to understand the scope of things, the ground below,
the ocean as it becomes one swelling,
unbroken heart.

To understand the boom-boom of the world
as the ones we've loved—fierce as tigers—vanish,
would be to disappear, too, and maybe that's why
in order to find new love we must do

what the test says we cannot.

NEW YORK CITY POEM

You didn't know it would be so beautiful, the way
a woman could say, "You don't need those" right after
you bought a pack of cigarettes. But most of all,
you didn't know you'd end up here, 27 years old
and waiting for a sign. You didn't know
that you would see a woman on the subway
dressed as a butterfly and think, "She is it."

You didn't know you would hear a man
riding a Brooklyn-bound train late at night
yell at you about how much he hates himself.
You didn't know you would hear yourself
reflected in his voice, the way he scared
you, the way you walked home shaking,
the way you searched for the moon
between row houses, the way that night
changed you.

You didn't know you would speak
to the woman dressed as a butterfly,
offer her your e-mail, telling her she's
magic. You didn't know she would never
respond. But you hoped—

You hoped, every single day for a sign
as you walked down Eastern Parkway,
understanding that each season was
passing, stepping in each moment
with both assurance and uncertainty.

You didn't know what waited for you
when you left your tropical home
for the big city, cold and sparkling.

You didn't know that your DNA
would spiral outward, like a heart
feels when it's falling in love.

But when you were in it, when you carried
yourself up and down subway tunnels, through
avenues and streets, you knew
there was kindness in the chaos.

The eye of the storm
finding itself.

TONIGHT IS

canvas, stereo boom, paint
to palette, mountainous—
and the artist, she is ready to shape me,
help me understand
that I am good enough
without the woman
who ran with me
like a wild horse.

And as she unwraps her brushes,
I wait, hoping that our experience
in this bare room of mine
can open something
within my heart,

can make room
for discovery,

can help me understand
I am the same as I've always been:

Hopeful—

a woman in a sparse room
with two suitcases,
a book of maps,

and that is good enough.

Yes, I am the same as I've always been:

A woman seeking solace
fresh from the shower,
cup of tea in my hands
waiting for you
to come out of your home
to meet me in this safe space
where trust is not an art, but inherent,

in this place where I can bare my body to you
open my legs wide
ready
to begin, to begin, to begin.

NOW IT'S HER TURN

THIS IS THE BEGINNING, AGAIN, AND HERE

SHE FINDS YOU

SHE PLACES HER HAND

ON YOUR STRONG HEART

SHE UNDERSTANDS THAT

THE TICK
TICK
TICK

WILL NOT LAST FOREVER

THAT SOMETHING, AT SOME POINT

WILL HAVE TO STOP

AND WHEN THAT TIME COMES

BECAUSE IT WILL

SHE REMEMBERS SOMETHING GREAT

SOMETHING BEAUTIFUL

SHE REMEMBERS YOU, THE FIRST WOMAN

TO EVER LOVE HER

SHE REMEMBERS HOW YOU KISSED
HER THIGHS,

HER HEART

HOW YOU MADE A NEST OF HER BODY

SHE REMEMBERS THE WAY
SHE LOVED YOU BACK

THE WAY YOU SAID, TO HER:

I SEE YOU

I SEE YOU

AND I AM HERE

DEDICATION:
TO THE WOMAN IN WINDOW LIGHT

Tell me, did you see it coming, the missile made to
destroy the world?

I am here to tell you a secret: When all of our roads
become rivers, that's when we'll all know it's time
to move, as gentle as we once were.

At one point in time, I believe we all shone bright
behind glass, not made to ease one great pain,
but created
to warm the Earth, to bring light to it, as our
loved ones dug
with rhythm, making music.

Thousands of years later, you will grab my hand and
ask me to dance.

And then, you will connect wires.

And then, we will build a nest.

I WAS A ROSE

and I said, to you, “Hold on.”
You wrapped your fingers
around my stem, and you
were careful, soft, as you
lifted me. “You are my rose,”
you said. You looked holy
through window light.

Later that day, I grew two legs,
and you became the ocean.

I ran to you, and one thick wave
curled over my body—like a dove’s
wing, or like a palm—and I remember
a time when you hushed a hurricane
with your hands.

As all good miracles go: Time passes, ocean
joins body. Ocean tugs deep. Body’s heart goes
one, two. Earth levels, splits. Body grows roots,
flowers. Ocean longs to remember its feet.

They say bodies change when a lover leaves.

Above me, an oak brings shade.

VI

AFTER TWO YEARS OF MOURNING

OVER 100 YEARS LATER, MY FAMILY GROWS

and we don't understand the great, beautiful
way wild geese begin—again—in fields of wheat,
but we try. The flock moves like one, peaceful hand

and I am reminded of the stillness
of it all, how I feel honored
to be just one beating heart

among many. We are not in Sicily,
but we are somewhere ancient,
somewhere hard—a place
with earned history.

I remember the way my body moved
into each subway car, onto each airplane,
and I feel expansive, whole—
even though so much is gone.

But so much is here: the way animal
becomes flower. I am in no hurry

to bloom: the sun is low

in the sky, almost set now.

Three deer jump over the fence
my cousin built, piece by piece.

The night's first window is lit:

and it's simple, as faint
as a candle, or as a sigh

of relief, of landing.

EASTER POEM

Begin.

Yes, it's that simple.

Our hands will turn to roses
and our feet to roots,

and we will not call it a miracle, no,
we will call it *change*, we will call it
soul work, and you will tell me
how heavy it felt to hold your kin
as he died, how wide the world became,
how different, how quiet.

In this quiet world, we will learn
to reveal ourselves, slowly, as each season
imprints, passes, and finally, finally drops—

like a lover letting go,

opening her palm—free,
steady.

A PRAYER FOR YOUR SAFE RETURN HOME

I've been praying
for the wrong thing: Her, returning
to me. Instead, I should have been
asking for a new hope, the way
birds take turns holding one another
during flight. I wonder, do the birds
ever get tired of leaving? Of moving
to a newness, a place of warmth?

You can't go home again.
I've been praying for the wrong thing.
Finally, this time,
when the currents of something greater
drop me into the holy beautiful mess
of things, I will now long for
nothing but present motion,
the way concrete presses to feet,
and the acceptance of this:

what returns
will be what returns
will be what returns,

and you may have never seen her before,
or you may have touched her
a million times.

Either way,
I have learned
to pray for the thing,
the sweetest thing
that will meet you
upon arrival.

AFTER TWO YEARS OF MOURNING

I dreamt of someone's mother.
She was alive and bright,
silent, present. She held me
in her light, gently,
as if she knew
it had been a long time
since my body
felt a kind touch.

When I woke,
my heart unraveled
like an angel falling
through panes of glass.

She said, *finally*.

I said, *I am ready now*.

IMAGINE: WIDE OPEN SPACE

WHERE ROSES SPROUT FROM DESERT ROCKS

THE WORLD IS ON FIRE

AND NO, YOU DO NOT HAVE TO BE GOOD[2]

2. Mary Oliver, "Wild Geese"

ALL YOU HAVE TO DO IS WAIT

HOLD YOURSELF

WRAP YOUR OWN ARMS
AROUND YOUR BARE BODY

PRAY IN POETRY

AND SOON

YOU WILL RECEIVE A LETTER
FROM A PERSON FAR

AND IT WILL HOLD

ONE IMAGE: A TORNADO
FROZEN OVER WATER

AND AS YOU BREATHE STEADILY

IN TIME, THIS PERSON WILL SEND YOU MORE

THIS PERSON WILL SEND YOU

PHOTOGRAPHS OF FLOODS

SANDSTORMS

LETTERS OF THEIR OWN LOSSES

YOU SEND THEM A PRINT OF

HAIL, DROPPING LIKE TREASURE

OR LIKE AN EGG, TUMBLING

INSIDE OF A SACRED SPACE

THIS PERSON SAYS THEY FOUND YOUR
ADDRESS IN A POEM

ON THE BACK OF A PIGEON

BUT THEY CAN'T REMEMBER WHICH POEM

THE ONE WHERE YOU DREAMED OF
HEALTH, MAYBE

THE ONE WHERE YOU WOKE UP NEW,
MAYBE

YOU SAY

WHERE CAN I FIND YOU?

AND THEY UNRAVEL, A WHITE FLAG AT DAYBREAK

YOU OPEN, AN EXPLOSION

SHH, THEY SAY

WE ARE JUST BEGINNING

ACKNOWLEDGEMENTS

These poems (or versions of these poems) have appeared in the following publications:

"Before it Breaks," *The Ampersand Review & The Iron Horse Literary Review Film Festival*

"When All the Wars in this World," "The Day They Found," "Flower Girl," "If I Become a Ghost," "Faith Story I," "Faith Story II," "If I Were Amelia Earhart," *Adrienne*

"I See You There in Black and White," (published under the title "Bomb"), *The Los Angeles Review*

"Through Yet Another War," "In A Simpler Time," *Paper Nautilus*

"County Line Poem," *The Good Men Project*

"Dedication: To The One I Will Marry," *Sweet: A Literary Confection*

"Atlantic," *Ultraviolet Tribe*

"To Be The Houses," & "At My Grandmother's Funeral, I Imagine Holding Hands With The Woman I Loved" (published under the title "At My Grandmother's Funeral, I Imagined Holding My Lover's Hand"), *Corium Magazine*

"Last Night in a Dream," *The Writing Disorder*

"I Was Never Afraid to Dream," "New York City Poem," "Burial," *OCHO*

"Dedication: To the Registrar," *PANK* blog

ASHLEY INGUANTA is the author of three collections: *The Way Home* (Dancing Girl Press, 2013), *For The Woman Alone* (Ampersand Books, 2014), and *Bomb*. Ashley is also the Art Director of *SmokeLong Quarterly* and a Contributing Editor at *The Writing Disorder*. She teaches writing and restorative yoga classes at several locations in Central Florida, and is currently at work on a series of art films and poetry performances with violinist Sarah Morrison.

CPSIA information can be obtained
at www.ICGtesting.com
Printed in the USA
LVOW12s0526140418
573474LV00002B/352/P

9 780986 137051